CW00570866

The St
the Royal Maundy

Peter A. Wright, CVO

Secretary of the Royal Almonry

ABOVE: *The Queen distributes the Royal Maundy at Birmingham Cathedral.*

LEFT: *The Maundy ceremony in the ante-chapel of the Chapel Royal, Whitehall, 1733, from a drawing by S. H. Grimm.*

The Maundy Prayer

*L*ord Jesus Christ, who before
instituting the Holy
Sacrament at thy last Supper,
washed the feet of thine
Apostles; teach us, by thine
example, the grace of humility;
and so cleanse us from all stain
of sin that we may worthily
partake of thy holy mysteries;
who with the Father and the
Holy Spirit art one God, world
without end.

Amen

Probably at no other time has the
Royal Maundy service gained such
widespread interest as it has today, and
this can be attributed not only to the
importance which The Queen has placed
upon the ceremony by attending in
person on so many occasions, but also
because the locale has varied from year
to year.

For several centuries the distribution
of Maundy gifts had been made in
London. After the closing of the old
Chapel Royal in Whitehall in 1890 the
service was held annually at Westminster Abbey for sixty years, with the
exception of the years 1911 and 1937
when the abbey was closed for coronation preparations and the gifts were
distributed in St Paul's Cathedral.

At the beginning of Queen Elizabeth
II's reign, however, it was to become the
custom in some years to hold the service
at places other than Westminster Abbey.
At first these venues were in or around
London but before long the ceremony
was to be witnessed by congregations

ABOVE: *The Queen and the Duke of Edinburgh, with Royal Almonry officials, outside Worcester Cathedral.*

RIGHT: *A unique miniature by Nicholas Hilliard of Queen Elizabeth I at a Maundy ceremony (c.1560).*

LEFT: *The red and white long-stringed leather purses are placed on the Maundy Dish by the Assistant Secretary of the Royal Almonry.*

in other parts of the country. One immediate effect resulting from this change was the necessity to revise the rule relating to the selection of recipients. Until 1952 it had been possible for the recipients, having been selected, to remain on the Maundy list for the rest of their lives. Now that the ceremony was to be observed in other areas, however, it became necessary to grant the Maundy gift to new applicants on the one occasion only.

Though the ceremonial has been subject to several changes since earlier times, and has been shorn of some of its original features, today's Royal Maundy service still bears a marked resemblance to those held in the reign of Elizabeth I.

Even in its present shortened form much has been preserved and it remains one of the most interesting and colourful of the ancient ceremonies.

The act of washing the feet was discontinued in the 18th century in this particular ceremony, but the officials still wear linen towels throughout the service. The towels, which resemble large white sheets, are now worn over the right shoulder and tied round the waist. Until about 1880 the linen worn by the officials was retained by all who appeared in it, but this privilege was then withdrawn and the linen is now returned to the Royal Almonry after use to be washed in readiness for the next occasion. The pieces of linen in use at the present time do in fact date back to 1883 and have been used in Maundy distributions ever since. Until 1936 linen towels were also worn by the four almonry children, but the only people who now wear the linen are the Lord High Almoner, Sub-Almoner, Secretary and Assistant Secretary.

Traditional nosegays are carried by the principal people taking part in the service and were originally a precaution against possible infection. The nosegays used nowadays are made up during the night prior to the service and are composed so as to present a dome-like appearance. They are larger than those of earlier times and usually include daffodils, cheerfulness, stock, violets, primroses, cupressus, thyme and rosemary. The nosegays carried by the four almonry children are slightly smaller.

During the opening processional hymn the alms dishes containing the purses of Maundy coins are placed on a table in the central passage of the sanctuary. The exhortation from St John's Gospel xiii: 34, 'A new Commandment have I given unto you that ye love one another as I have loved you', is then delivered. The first lesson recalls the story of Christ washing the feet of the apostles (St John xiii) and the second

lesson contains the passage from St Matthew xxv about the Last Judgment. In addition to the inclusion of two hymns and a psalm, a number of anthems are sung at various points during the service, in particular when the distributions are in progress, and these usually include 'Lord for thy tender mercies' sake' by Hilton, 'Wash me

ABOVE: *The Secretary of the Royal Almonry and the Yeomen of the Guard play supporting roles in the distribution of the Royal Maundy.*

ABOVE: *The Queen and the Duke of Edinburgh both hold traditional nosegays of spring flowers and herbs, originally an attempt to ward off disease.*

throughly from my wickedness' by Wesley and Handel's 'Zadok the Priest'.

The qualifying age for a Maundy recipient is 65, but the average age of those attending is usually between 80 and 85. Recipients are recommended by clergy and ministers from within the boundary of the diocese in which the Maundy Service is held. The nominations come from Anglican, Roman Catholic and the Free Churches, and from the Salvation Army. During recent years efforts have been made to involve as many Christian churches as possible.

The recipients who share in the service may not always be aware of the historical background to Royal Maundy. The gifts which they receive bear little relation in value to those given in former times. But these people are chosen because of what they themselves have tried to do for others, and they share with all a knowledge of the new commandment given at the Last Supper, from which this ceremony has come down to us. Indeed the most impressive moment in the entire service is without doubt when the Sovereign walks the length of the choir and into the nave to make the distribution of gifts – a symbol of the simple act of grace portraying the compassion and humility of Our Lord.

The story of the Royal Maundy is one of the most interesting of ancient ceremonies. Though much of its early history is veiled in obscurity there can be no doubt as to its origin. Those who collect the sets of specially minted Maundy money do not always realise that the coins are associated with a ceremony based entirely on an incident which occurred on the night before Our Lord's crucifixion. St John recalls that immediately after the Last Supper, Jesus laid aside his garments, girded himself with a towel, poured water into a basin, and then in turn he washed the feet of his disciples. Afterwards he delivered to them a command, or *mandatum*, for his followers to love one another, and said: 'I have given you an example that ye should do as I have done to you.'

It is from the Latin *mandatum* that the word Maundy derives.

The Mandatum

The simple and gracious act of humility which Our Lord performed on this occasion is still recalled regularly by Christian churches in many lands. In the Church of the Holy Sepulchre in Jerusalem the Patriarch of the Greek Orthodox Church washes the right foot of twelve senior clerics – who represent the apostles – while the story is intoned. The Armenians also hold a similar service, in the form of a mass, in their cathedral of St James in the old city. In Rome Pope John XXIII restored the custom of washing feet on Maundy Thursday after a lapse of some ninety years, and subsequent Popes have continued the practice. A similar service used to be performed at Moscow by the archbishop. In Austria, the emperor, assisted by the archdukes of the blood royal, served a repast of many courses to twelve old men, and washed their feet. In Spain, at Seville, it was customary for the archbishop to give a splendid cold dinner to twelve paupers, and then

receive them at the cathedral, where the ablution ceremonies were performed with much pomp. Similar services are held every year in Roman Catholic cathedrals throughout the world.

Seventh-day Adventists observe the ceremony on the twelfth sabbath day of each quarter. The service is known as the ordinance of humility and the men and women take part separately. It is suggested that participants correct misunderstandings and confess their faults to one another at this service. Afterwards men and women come together for holy communion, in the main body of the church.

In England the Maundy is referred to by St Augustine *c.* AD 600. The rite can be traced back to the *pedilavium* or washing of the feet of the 5th century which followed holy communion on Maundy Thursday. Indeed the ceremony of the

ABOVE: *The seal of Henry de Bluntesdon (King's Almoner c.1284–1305) bears the inscription* Sigillian Servi Dei *(Seal in the service of God) and depicts the Almoner distributing alms from a basket to an eager crowd who wait with outstretched arms. This is the earliest known representation of the King's Almoner distributing Maundy alms to the poor.*

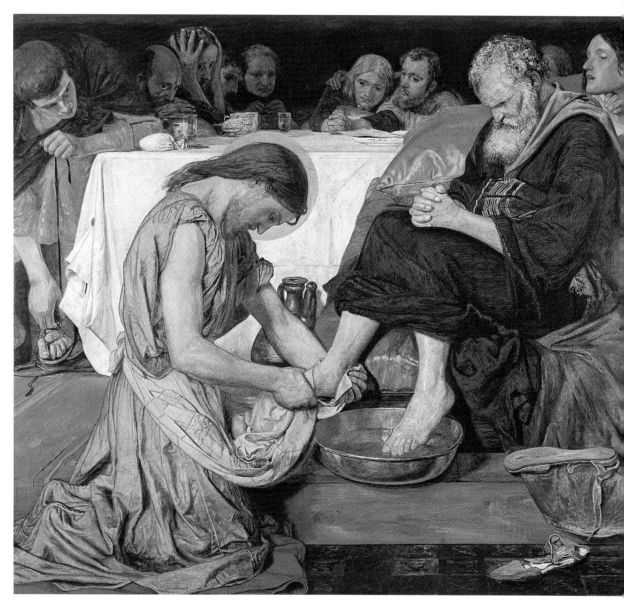

ABOVE: *Ford Madox Brown's painting,* Jesus Washing Peter's Feet – *the incident in the New Testament upon which the Maundy ceremony is based.*

washing of the feet of the poor was not limited to that day alone in the early Church, and prior to the Norman Conquest the *pedilavium* was performed daily in some monasteries.

There are many Anglican and Roman Catholic churches in Britain today where the feet washing ceremony is observed on Maundy Thursday.

Royal Maundy

King John is known to have taken part in the Maundy ceremony at Knaresborough in Yorkshire in 1210, and also at Rochester in Kent in 1213 where he gave thirteen pence to each of thirteen men. During the 14th century it seems to have been the custom for most members of the royal family to be present on Maundy Thursday in order to distribute gifts of money and clothing to thirteen men. Henry IV, however, began the practice of relating the number of recipients to the sovereign's age so that the number would gradually increase during the reign.

It is because it became the custom for the sovereign to perform this ceremony that the event came to be known as the Royal Maundy, and those to whom this service was rendered were the aged poor. To the ordinary ceremony of that day, therefore, was gradually added gifts of clothing, food and money, to which the name Maundy was given.

In some accounts of the ceremony it is stated that the sovereign kissed the feet of the poor people and gave them the gowns they were wearing. The *Venetian Calendar* contained a long account, written by Cardinal Pole's secretary, of Queen Mary I's great fervour in carrying out this fatiguing rite in 1556 and in taking special trouble to find the most worthy recipient for her gown of the finest purple cloth, lined with martens' fur, with sleeves 'so long and wide they reached the ground'. After going the whole length of the hall 'from one end to the other ever on her knees' in the ceremony of washing the women's feet, the Queen went twice round the hall, examining very closely all the poor women one by one, and then returning for the third time 'she gave the said gown to the one who was in fact the poorest and most aged of them all'. The number of women to whom the service was performed corresponded with the years of the sovereign and is given correctly as forty-one. The sixth time the Queen went round the hall 'she gave a leathern purse, containing forty-one pennies, according to the number of her own years, and which in value may amount to rather more than half an Italian golden crown . . .'.

Regarding the presentation of the royal gown it is interesting to note that on 19 March 1572 Elizabeth I is recorded by William Lambarde as substituting a money gift in a red purse for her gown 'which (so men say) by ancient order she ought to give to some of them at her pleasure'. This alteration was caused 'to avoid trouble of suite, which accustomabile was made for that perferment' (preferment). She had, therefore, 'changed the rewarde into money to be equally divided amongst them all, namely 20s apiece'.

In ransoming her gown Elizabeth was reverting to the custom of her little brother Edward, whose childish robes were redeemed at 20s. to each of the twelve men to whom he also presented ten pence in his first regnal year. This payment continues to be made as redemption money and forms part of the Maundy given to each recipient.

A detailed account of the 1572 ceremony states that the Queen took part in a grand Maundy ceremonial in the Hall at Greenwich, where the recipients were duly assembled. A cushion was placed in front of each person for Elizabeth to kneel upon, and her chaplain conducted the service. First the laundress, who was provided with a silver basin containing warm water and sweet flowers, washed the feet of the poor people, and then, after the singing of a hymn, the Sub-Almoner and the Lord High Almoner in turn repeated the process. The chaplain read the lesson describing the washing of the disciples' feet, and then the Queen entered the hall, attended by thirty-nine ladies and gentlemen – the number corresponding to the years of her age. The 'gentlefolks' put on aprons, and bearing towels and basins of water and sweet flowers, waited on the Queen who washed, crossed and kissed the feet of the poor women, as the laundress, the Sub-Almoner and the Lord High Almoner had done before her. She then distributed the presents: broadcloth with which to make gowns, a pair

ABOVE: *A pen and wash drawing by S. H. Grimm of the Almonry Procession in 1773. It shows the nosegays, the way the towels were then worn and the Alms Dish being carried, as now, on the head of a Yeoman of the Guard.*

of sleeves, a wooden platter upon which was half a side of salmon, the same amount of ling, six red herrings, and six loaves of 'cheat-bread' together with a white wooden dish of claret wine. She also bestowed on the poor women the towels she had used and the aprons worn by the attendants. The long ceremonial was then at an end, and the Queen took her departure. This interesting record concludes with the timely observation 'by now the sun was setting'.

From itemised accounts of her almoner in 1582, it is expressly stated that 'by Her Highnes owne handes' she gave to forty-eight women 'fortie-eight pens in memorye of Her M. aige'. Moreover, it is recorded that the money was given 'to every pore woman in a whyte purse and to the said women in a redd purse Twentye shillings in lieu of Her M. owne gowne, the purses costing the unusually large sum of 13d. a doz.'. We also find a very detailed description by an eye-witness on 17 April 1595, when the office 'of the Queenes Maundaye was performed' by 'Dr. Mathewes Bisshop of Durhm', the prelate 'washing the right foot of 57 severell women' and giving to each a 'redd purse and a whyt, as they say

40s therein'. If the date is correct, the number of women should have been sixty-two and the two gifts of money £1 5s. 2d.

A miniature painted by Nicholas Hilliard shows Elizabeth, followed by Blanche Parry, her principal lady-in-waiting, and various members of the court. The officiating clergy, the children of the Almonry, and, finally, a large number of poor persons, are delineated here. So excellent is the portraiture that Blanche Parry is recognizable by the comparison with her picture at Hampton Court and her monument in St Margaret's, Westminster; and yet the hundred or more figures are represented in a space measuring only 70 by 57mm. This miniature has been approximately dated to the year 1560, and the style of dress corresponds with this assumption. It is thought to represent the almsgiving on 11 April 1560, described by Nichols in his *Progress of Queen Elizabeth*.

It is known that in Tudor, and earlier times, the queen-consorts gave their Maundy, but there are few detailed records of the wives of the Stuart kings performing this office. One of the acts of tyranny of Henry VIII was to forbid Catherine of Aragon to 'keep her Maundy' after he divorced her, but when 'the Princess Dowager' as she was termed by him, declared her intention of doing so 'in spite of the king's order last year to the contrary', Henry gave a qualified consent by stating 'The King is content if she does not keep it as Queen; if so, she and others would be guilty of High Treason'.

It was quite usual for other than royal personages at that time to give Maundy doles. Wolsey and other prelates and great noblemen, such as the Earl of Northumberland, did so; but generally this was a distribution to twelve persons only to represent the apostles.

During the Civil War, Charles I did not fail to 'keep his Maundy'. Christopher Hildyard chronicles the king's visit to York on 30 March 1639 on his way up to Scotland. But the distribution was made 'for' the king on 11 April:

On Maundy Thursday, Doctor Curle, Bishop of Winchester, the King's Almoner, kept the Maundy in the Minster giving as the King's gift to nine and thirty poor men each of them four yards of Holland, three yards of Broad Cloth, a pair of Shoes, a Wooden Platter with a Jowle of Ling and another of Salmon, six Red Herrings, two loaves of Bread, a scale of Wine, twenty Shillings in Money, nine and thirty single Pence, and washed their feet.

Again in 1642, Hildyard briefly states: 'This year His Majesty kept his Maundy in the Minster upon the Seventh of April.' Charles was then in his forty-second year.

Charles I, like some of his predecessors, had refrained from personally performing the ceremonial rite of feet washing owing to an outbreak of the plague. Charles II, on the other hand, and despite the plague, had courted the utmost popularity by resuming the old established custom of 'personal service'. In his revival of the personal ministra-

tion, Charles II also restored the service of the distribution.

Mention is made of the 1685 ceremony in a small book kept at the office of the Registrar-General at Somerset House and entitled 'Chapels Royal Register – Births, Deaths, Marriages':

On Maundy Thursday, April 16th 1685, our gracious King James ye 2nd was'd, wip'd, and kiss'd the feet of 52 poor men with wonderful humility. And all the Service of the Church of England usuall on that occasion was perform'd, his Majesty being present all the time.

The observance of the practice in the English court is also attested by Delaune (1690):

On the Thursday before Easter, called Maundy Thursday, the King or his Lord High Almoner, assisted by the Sub-Almoner, was wont to wash the feet of as many poor men as His Majesty had reigned years, and then to wipe them with a towel (according to the pattern of our Saviour). After this he gave every one of them two and a half yards of woollen cloth with which to make a suit of clothes; also linen cloth for two shirts, as well as a pair of stockings and a pair of shoes; three dishes of fish in wooden platters, one of salt salmon, a second of green fish or cod, a third of pickle-herrings – red herrings or red sprats – a gallon of beer, a quart bottle of wine, and four sixpenny loaves of bread, also a red leather purse with as many single pence as the King is years old, and in such another purse as many shillings as the King had reigned years. The Queen doth the like to diverse poor persons.

Had it not been for the real piety and earnestness with which the ceremony was usually undertaken in those days of simple faith, the physical fatigue of the ministrations would have tried the patience of all participators in the service. To the aged and infirm the strain of carrying out the office was great, especially as, to the most saintly,

ABOVE: *An engraving by James Basire of Grimm's drawing of the 1773 Maundy ceremony in progress in the old Chapel Royal in Whitehall.*

the performance involved traversing the hall kneeling. It is indeed told of St Oswald, Archbishop of York, that 'he passed to the Lord' in AD 922 'whilst according to the usual custom he was observing the usual Maundy before the feet of the poor'.

Original copies of the *Protestant Mercury* in the Bodleian Library at Oxford provide the following information about the Maundy ceremony of 1698: 'Yesterday being Maundy Thursday, His Majesty came to the Banqueting House from Kensington, and washed the feet of twelve poor men; and gave them money, and cloth to make them garments.' Why the number of recipients should not have corresponded with the age of the sovereign on this occasion is not known, but it does seem that William III would have been one of the last monarchs to wash the feet.

In 1724 an alteration was made to the ceremony, and the women were now to receive a money allowance instead of clothing. The reason alleged for this change was that as the garments were of a feminine nature, and not made to measure, the recipients showed an eager desire to see if the gifts fitted them, thus creating a most unseemly bustle. From later records it appears that clothing was again distributed for a while to the women in the form of material instead of ready-made articles.

The following account of the 1731 ceremony is recorded in Walford's *Old and New London*:

On the 5th April 1731, it being Maundy Thursday, the King then being in his 48th year, there was distributed at the Banqueting House, Whitehall, to 48 poor men and 48 poor women, boiled beef and shoulders of mutton, and small bowls of ale, which is called dinner; after that, large wooden platters of fish and loaves, viz. undressed, one large ling and one large dried cod; twelve red herrings and twelve white herrings; and four quartern loaves. Each person had one platter of this provision; after which was distributed to them, shoes, stockings, linen and woollen cloth, and leathern bags, with onepenny, twopenny, threepenny and fourpenny pieces of silver, and shillings, to each about £4 in value. His Grace The Lord Archbishop of York, Lord High Almoner, also performed the annual ceremony of washing the feet of the poor in the Royal Chapel, Whitehall, as formerly done by the Kings themselves.

It will be seen that on this occasion the Maundy recipients did not receive the £1 which Elizabeth I and her successors had given in redemption of the gowns worn by them on the day of distribution. The men received the provisions, silver pennies and clothing, and the women the provisions, silver pennies and a money allowance in lieu of clothing. This continued until 1759 when the £1 was again restored.

During the 18th and 19th centuries the ceremony was held in the antechapel of the Chapel Royal, Whitehall. Three drawings by S. H. Grimm of the 1773 ceremony are most interesting, and in one of them the loaves and the fish are clearly seen. The drawing of the procession into the chapel reveals that in those times the linen towels were girded round the waist whereas they are now also worn over the right shoulder. The nosegays of earlier times were smaller and the purse strings shorter than those used in present-day ceremonies.

A short account of the 1802 distribution states that as many poor men and women as the king was years of age sat down at two tables in Whitehall Chapel and were waited on by his attendants. Each person received a ration of beef of about four pounds (1.8 kg) in weight and four threepenny loaves. A cup of ale was then given to them and they departed with cheerful hearts. In the afternoon clothes and money were distributed. The proceedings covered several hours of the day and great store was set on the various provisions given.

In 1814 there were one hundred and fifty Maundy recipients:

In the morning the Sub-Almoner, the Secretary of the Lord High Almoner, and others belonging to the Lord Chamberlain's office, attended by a party of the Yeomen of the Guard, distributed to 75 poor women and 75 poor men, being as many as the King was years old, a quantity of salt fish consisting of salmon, cod, herrings, and pieces of very fine beef, 5 loaves of bread and some ale to drink the King's health . . . A procession entered of those engaged in the ceremony, consisting of a party of the Yeomen of the Guard, one of them carrying on his head a large gold dish, containing 150 bags, with 75 silver pennies in each for the poor people, which was placed in the Royal Closet. They were followed by the Sub-Almoner in his robes, with a sash of fine linen over his shoulder and crossing his waist. He was followed by two boys, two girls, the Secretary and other gentlemen all carrying nosegays. The Church Evening Service was then performed, at the conclusion of which the silver pennies were distributed, and woollen cloth, linen, shoes and stockings to the men and women, and a cup of wine to drink the King's health.

It was on this occasion that due to the preparation for a concert arranged under the auspices of Queen Charlotte the ante-chapel was not available. A lean-to was therefore erected against the wall of the chapel facing Whitehall Gardens and extending the whole length of the side of the building. This temporary structure was fitted up with forms, tables and other necessaries. Every effort was made to ensure the comfort of the many recipients and it was used on every subsequent occasion for the same purpose until 1837 when the festival, or would-be dinner, was dispensed with. The reason for this was that the recipients often sold the provisions given to them for a trifling sum, amounts even as low as five shillings

ABOVE: *The crossbelts on the uniforms of the Yeomen of the Guard show that they are members of The Queen's Bodyguard and distinguish them from the Yeomen Warders of the Tower of London.*

having been paid for them. As the contract price was thirty shillings a head William IV sanctioned a money allowance in lieu of the provisions.

A further alteration in the form of the bounty was made in 1883 when a money allowance was paid to each man in lieu of clothing. The reason for this change was not the same as that already recorded in the case of the women. Except for trying to exchange shoes, the men were content to take away their gifts without inspection, but they were often unable to afford the expense of having the materials made up into clothing.

In 1890 the Royal Chapel in Whitehall was handed over to the Royal United Services Institution, and from 1891 for an almost unbroken period of sixty years the Maundy ceremony made Westminster Abbey its new home. As the various gifts in kind had now been replaced by monetary gifts, the emphasis quite rightly centred more on the message and meaning of the service itself. Though the Maundy ceremony had been witnessed from time to time by various members of the royal family, no reigning monarch had actually taken

part in it for more than two centuries and the distribution had therefore been made either by the Lord High Almoner or the Sub-Almoner. In 1932, however, King George V restored the custom and attended the abbey in person to hand the traditional red and white purses to the recipients in the second distribution.

It was during the latter part of this reign that green and white purses with short strings were introduced into the service and were used for the gifts in lieu of clothing. Prior to this the clothing money given in the first distribution had been handed to the recipients in a form of pay packet which was taken from a silken pouch. After 1979 the short-stringed purses were withdrawn and the clothing gift is now included in the red purse with long white strings.

In 1935 The Queen – then Princess Elizabeth – first attended the service. In 1936 King Edward VIII distributed the gifts, and King George VI distributed the Maundy on seven occasions.

The tradition of the Royal Maundy distribution has been continued by The Queen, and the service is now held in different parts of the country.

13

The Maundy Money

Manuscripts preserved at the Public Record Office and the British Museum and the records of the Privy Council contain much information concerning the number of special coins.

The various charities required mainly the half-groat and the silver penny, and often the fourpenny coins now included under the name of Maundy. But it was the silver penny alone which was used by the Tudors and Stuarts for the special ceremony on Holy Thursday, when the monarch gave a penny for each year of his age, with an added year of grace, to the same number of poor persons.

On 2 April 1574 (Maundy Thursday was on 8 April in that year) 10 lb (4.5 kg) of silver, roughly speaking enough to make £30 worth of small coin, was ordered to be coined into 'single pennies'

at the rate of 720 to the pound Troy, and of 11 oz 2 dwt (315 g) fine silver for Elizabeth's private use. In the year 1576, in the *Acts of the Council* '18th April Mr. Martin, officer of the Mint, to deliver £12 in pence for H.M's. service on Maundy Thursday'. (The order must have been designed to meet the requirements of the following day, 19 April, and shows that the money was in some already prepared stock.) Again, nearly two years later, 18 March 1578, 'Warrant to Warden of the Mint for delivery of £13 in new pence for Maundy'. (In 1578 the day of distribution was on 27 March.) From these orders it is apparent that about 10s. of pence were added year by year to meet the increasing age of Elizabeth, who would in 1578 require £8 8s. 9d. (that is to say, 2025 pennies at 45 times 45, as against 43 times 43 in 1576).

ABOVE: *Two sets of Maundy money showing obverse and reverse sides. The face value of a set of Maundy coins is equal to 10p.*

The Maundy money as it is known today started with an undated issue of hammered coinage attributed to Charles II in 1662. The coins were in four, three, two and one penny denominations. This first issue can be recognized by the bust of the monarch inside an inner circle. A second undated set by Thomas Simon appeared the following year and featured the bust extending to the edge of the coin. The first dated Maundy coin was a two-penny piece made in the reign of Charles II in 1668, and 1670 is the earliest date that contains a full set of groat, threepenny, half-groat and penny.

Until 1821, however, the issuance of Maundy money was irregular, but by the end of the century the sets had become so plentiful that anyone in England who could afford a bank account could order a set of Maundy coins. This abusive service was discontinued in 1909, and there is now a greater control over the number of coins actually struck. In addition to the sets of coins given to the Maundy recipients, other sets are distributed as fees to those who either officiate in the ceremony or who have had some share in the preparations for it.

The following extract from the 77th annual report of the Deputy Master and Comptroller of the Royal Mint for the year 1946 is of interest. In referring to the cessation of the manufacture of silver coins the report says: 'The use of silver in English coinage, which has been continuous since the seventh century, is not, however, to disappear entirely, the decision, welcome to scholars and aesthetes, having been taken to resume the use of the sterling standard in Maundy Money, the silver penny, twopence, threepence and fourpence.

BELOW: *The traditional red and white purses with long strings are made of soft leather and in the same style as those of earlier times.*

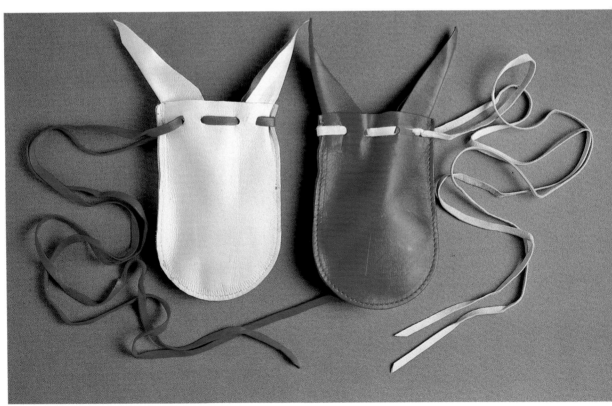

LEFT: *The silver-gilt Maundy Dish, upon which the purses are carried, was made in 1660 but is engraved with the cipher of William and Mary.*

BELOW: *The altar dishes known as the Fish Dishes are used to supplement the Maundy Dish for the distribution of the Royal Maundy.*

Of these coins, the English silver penny was instituted about AD 760, and gave its later name of the sterling to our whole currency system. . . . All were struck in sterling silver (silver of 925 millesimal fineness), with one brief interruption on Henry VIII's debasement of all coinage, until the general change in 1920, in which these small coins were included with the rest. The Act of 1946 thus restores to their ancient standard all those silver coins which antedate the discovery of argentiferous America, with the addition of the threepence when struck for use in the Maundy Service, while all those introduced after that date, including the threepence if required for circulation, are converted to cupro-nickel.'

The Maundy coins, being current coin of the realm, are of course legal tender, but as they are eagerly sought after by collectors they rarely pass into general use. Indeed, most Maundy recipients prefer to retain their coins as a personal treasure.

When the United Kingdom changed to decimal currency on 15 February 1971, the face value of a set of four Maundy coins became 10 new pence instead of 10d under the old £sd system. It was decided, however, that the new effigy which had been prepared for use on the decimal coins should not be applied to Maundy money.

The Purses

In earlier times the white purses containing the Maundy coins would have been tawed (alum-dressed) sheep or goat skin and hand-sewn. In the last century the purses were often made by poor children in the industrial schools. The modern purses are machine-sewn and the alumed leather has been superseded by new methods which produce a leather better in many respects than the ancient type. In size and style, however, these purses bear a close resemblance to their predecessors though they now cost considerably more than the 'unusually large sum of 13d. a dozen' referred to in the 16th century.

During the ceremony the Sovereign hands to each recipient two purses which are tied together with long leather strings. The red purse contains £3 in place of clothing which was given in earlier times, £1.50 for provisions and £1 for the redemption of the royal gown, making a total of £5.50. The white purse with the long red strings contains the silver Maundy coins, in sets, and consisting of the same number of pence as the Sovereign has years. Because of the historical associations the amounts distributed have varied little from earlier centuries, but the gifts are highly prized by recipients for to be included in the list is considered very much an honour.

The Alms Dishes

The silver-gilt Maundy Dish used in the first distribution is part of the regalia, and can normally be seen in the Jewel House at the Tower of London. Although the dish bears the cipher of William and Mary, it was given by Charles II and was actually made in 1660. The dish has a maker's mark of an orb and star on a plain shield; it weighs 5.7 kg and measures 64 cm in diameter.

The two altar dishes, used for the first time in 1971 for the second distribution also date from the time of Charles II and were once part of the Chapel Plate. They were added to the collection in the Jewel House at the Tower of London in 1967. They are commonly referred to as the Fish Dishes, one dish featuring seafish and the other freshwater fish, and individual species of fish of varying sizes are clearly recognizable. On the rims are four oval panels representing on one dish Love, Death, Industry and Strength, and on the other dish Faith, Hope, Justice and Fortitude.

Those who officiate annually in the Maundy Ceremony are carrying out roles which are steeped in tradition and history.

The Lord High Almoner

The Lord High Almoner is appointed by letters patent under the Great Seal, and it is his duty to be in attendance on, or represent, the Sovereign at the Maundy service. It has been possible to trace the names of High Almoners to the early 12th century, and it seems certain that during the 13th century there were at times two or even three almoners in office at the same period.

In the reign of Edward I it was the duty of the High Almoner to collect the fragments from the royal table and distribute them daily to the poor, to visit the sick, prisoners, poor widows and others in distress. He also had to remind the King about the bestowal of his alms and ensure that the valuable cast-off robes were not bestowed on players, minstrels or flatterers.

By the 15th century the office had increased in dignity and in 1440 John de la Bere was granted the office of 'Great Almoner' for life. Cardinal Wolsey kept his first Maundy celebration at Peterborough and is recorded to have given three white and three red herrings to each recipient. There is in existence at Hardwicke Court near Gloucester a Lord High Almoner's purse in green satin and gold lace. The purse belonged to Bishop Lloyd who was Lord High Almoner to William and Mary, and to whom it is believed the purse was given by Queen Anne.

In the reign of George II, Chamberlayne records in his *Present State of Great Britain* 1755, that:

> The Lord High Almoner disposes of the King's Alms, and for that use receives (besides other moneys allowed by the King) all deodands, and *bona felonum de*

se to be in that way disposed. Moreover, the Lord High Almoner hath the privilege to give the King's dish to whatsoever poor men he pleased; that is, the first dish at dinner which is set upon the King's table, or instead thereof 4d. per diem. Next he distributes to twenty-four poor men, nominated by the parishioners of the parish adjacent to the King's Palace of residence, to each of them 4d. in money, a twopenny loaf, and a gallon of beer, or instead thereof 3d. in money to be equally divided among them every morning at seven of the clock at the court-gate; and every poor man, before he receives the Alms, is to repeat the Creed and the Lord's Prayer in the presence of one of the King's Chaplains deputed by the Lord Almoner to be his Sub-Almoner; who is also to scatter new-coined two-pences in the towns and places where the King passeth through in his progress, to a certain sum by the year.

ABOVE: *The purse of Bishop William Lloyd, Lord High Almoner to King William III from 1689 to 1702.*

Partly because the Royal Almonry remained in Whitehall after it had ceased to be a royal residence, the office became less immediately associated with the Sovereign and the duties of the Lord High Almoner dwindled in importance. The Royal Almonry has, however, remained part of the Royal Household and is now allied to the Privy Purse at Buckingham Palace. The Lord High Almonership continues as an office of great dignity and one which has always been held by one of the higher clergy. Apart from a small fee paid in Maundy coins for attendance at the service there are no emoluments attached to the office of Lord High Almoner, though in earlier times the almoner had the right to occupy an official residence in Scotland Yard and also a number of personal privileges.

The present seal of the Royal Almoner depicts a three-masted ship in full sail. At first glance it might be difficult to see why such a seemingly inappropriate device was adopted, but it is thought to stem from the seal of Stephen Payne who was almoner to Henry V from 1414 to 1419. This seal depicts the almoner standing under a canopy and holding in his arms a model ship on wheels. An almsbox in the form of a ship on wheels, which could be rolled round a table, has been referred to in a later century. It would seem probable, therefore, that in course of time the original significance was forgotten, and there emerged a ship – without wheels – which came to be accepted as the official seal of the Royal Almonry and which still appears on all Almonry correspondence.

Stephen Payne came from County Durham, and even today there is a hospital in West Hartlepool which uses an emblem identical to his seal. The words 'sigill eleemosyn' on the present seal mean 'by sign (or symbol) of the Almonry'. Dean's Yard at Westminster Abbey was formerly the site of many monastic buildings including a brewhouse, granary and almonry. There was an old chapel by the almonry against which Henry VIII's mother erected an almshouse. This area was in fact originally called 'eleemosynary' or 'almonry'.

The Sub-Almoner

It has been possible to compile a complete list of those who have held the office of Sub-Almoner from about the middle of the 18th century, but for the earlier period the list is incomplete. In earlier days the appointment of a Sub-Almoner seems to have been seldom recorded officially except when referred to occasionally as 'the King's Under (or Sub) Almoner'. Since the beginning of this century the Sub-Almoner has also undertaken the duties of 'Sub-Dean of Her Majesty's Chapels Royal, Deputy Clerk of the Closet and Domestic Chaplain'. This affords a link between the Royal Almonry and the Chapel Royal as the Maundy Ceremony is still regarded as a Chapel Royal service.

RIGHT: *The Queen and the Duke of Edinburgh leave Birmingham Cathedral after the distribution of the Royal Maundy.*

LEFT: *The Maundy ceremony is a Chapel Royal service and even though it is no longer held in the Chapel Royal, the choir still attends on the Sovereign. Shown here are the Organist, the six Gentlemen of the Choir, the ten Children of the Choir and the Serjeant of the Vestry.*

LEFT: *The Children of the Chapel Royal Choir are all scholars at the City of London School. Their splendid clothing is of traditional design.*

The Secretary of the Royal Almonry and the Assistant Secretary

The Secretary of the Royal Almonry and the Assistant Secretary arrange for the various distributions of gifts at Easter from the funds of the Royal Almonry, and are responsible for the general preparations for the Maundy ceremony. During the service they assist in the distributions by indicating the various recipients to the Sovereign and taking the purses from the alms dish which the Yeoman carries. At the 1968 ceremony in Westminster Abbey the Secretary and the Assistant Secretary wore for the first time special gowns bearing the ancient Royal Almonry crest dating back to the 15th-century seal of Stephen Payne.

In addition to the Maundy gifts, the Royal Almonry still distributes small grants under the heading of Gate Alms, payments which themselves have an interesting history.

The Children of the Royal Almonry

At one time the Children of the Royal Almonry were not children at all, but were in fact old men. Their names are entered in the Almonry records prior to the year 1808 and their duties were to attend at the Chapel Royal on Maundy Thursday arrayed in linen scarves. Their fees in the aggregate amounted to £21 for this service. This was considered an abuse of the charity and eventually the men were replaced by real children, two girls and two boys. The attendance of these children serves as a reminder of the men who used to assist at the feet washing ceremony. The children, who are recommended from local schools, carry a nosegay during the ceremony and receive a 'fee' in the form of a set of Maundy money for their services.

The Wandsmen

The date of origin and the function performed by the six Wandsmen, or wandbearers as they were once called, is not definitely known. Their wands may have been willows or palms and thus be connected with the Easter festival, they may have been staves with which the populace were held back to make way for the recipients, or merely badges of office. Whatever their original function, however, the duty of the Wandsmen of the present day is to ensure that the recipients are present and seated in their proper places on either side of the choir and in the nave, explain to them their part in the service and to help them in every way possible.

The Maundy Recipients

From the 15th century the number of Maundy Recipients has been related to the years of the Sovereign's life. At one time the recipients were required to be of the same sex as the Sovereign, but

LEFT: *The Clerk of the Chapel, Buckingham Palace, leads the distribution of Maundy gifts while the Secretary of the Royal Almonry indicates the recipient to The Queen.*

ABOVE: *An 82-year-old recipient displays her Maundy gifts with pride.*

ABOVE RIGHT: *The Duke of Edinburgh holds a traditional nosegay as he leaves Worcester Cathedral after the Maundy ceremony.*

since the 18th century they have numbered as many men and women as the Sovereign has years of age. In earlier times preference was given to those in financial need, but the recipients are now recommended because of the Christian service they have given to the Church and the community.

The Chapel Royal Choir

One of the picturesque features of the Maundy service is the appearance of the Chapel Royal Choir, the children in their gold-braided red tunics, red breeches, white lace bands and white gloves, black stockings and shoes, all harmonizing with the uniforms of the Yeomen of the Guard. The gentlemen of the choir wear red cassocks with surplices and white ties. The origin of the choir, which would accompany the Sovereign on his journeyings with his retinue, goes back to a distant date, and it remains a distinctive part of the royal establishment. That it sang at Agincourt and that it was present at 'The Field of the Cloth of Gold' indicate the place it took in the royal entourage. The ancient custom of the choir's attendance upon

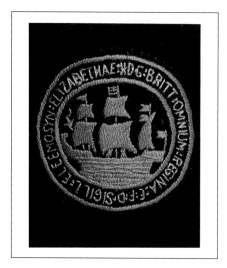

the Sovereign survives in the command it receives to sing at the Maundy service, and it has taken its part wherever the service has been held. It was in attendance too at the baptisms of the royal children as well as at royal weddings. The Chapel Royal Choir has a notable musical history, and its members value the proud inheritance into which they have entered.

The Yeomen of the Guard

The Yeomen of the Guard also play an important part in the Maundy distribution. The Queen's Bodyguard is the oldest military corps now existing in this or any other country. It was created by Henry VII from his band of faithful English and Welsh followers who had accompanied him in his exile in France and who marched with him to Bosworth Field, where he defeated and slew Richard III and was himself proclaimed King in 1485. At his coronation he announced that the guard was not only for his personal protection, but for 'The upholding of the dignity and grandeur of the English crown in perpetuity, his successors, the Kings and Queens of England for all time' – and so from that date to this the Yeomen of the Guard

have attended their Sovereigns at their coronations, have faithfully served them during their reigns, on their deaths have guarded their lying-in-state, and finally have escorted them reverently to their graves.

At first the Guard were virtually the personal servants of the Sovereign accompanying him everywhere in public and in private, and responsible for his safety even in battle, but after the year 1743 (the last occasion on which an English king fought in person), the duties of the Yeomen became purely ceremonial. The original duties of cooking, testing the food, making the King's bed, remaining on duty while the King slept are still commemorated by the fact that the duty officer and certain Yeomen stand behind the Sovereign's chair at State banquets, and by the appointment of certain senior Yeomen as Yeomen Bed-Goer (YBG) and Yeomen Bed-Hanger (YBH) in the roll of the Guard. Duties now performed by the Guard include the searching of the vaults of the Houses of Parliament two hours before the official opening by the Sovereign, lining the Royal Gallery of the House of Lords for the State Opening of Parliament, the Epiphany and Maundy services, the services of the Order of the Garter and of the Bath, guards of honour over the Sovereign in Buckingham Palace on the arrival of all foreign royalty or Heads of State on State visits, together with attendances at State banquets, investitures, garden parties etc. A roll of candidates for the Guard is maintained by the Ministry of Defence, and candidates are chosen from all regiments and corps of the Army, from the Royal Air Force and from the Royal Marines.

There are eighty men in the Queen's Bodyguard, about two dozen of whom, together with the adjutant, undertake duty in the Maundy service. Three of the Yeomen are responsible for carrying the dishes containing the Alms.

LEFT: *The badge worn by the Secretary of the Royal Almonry on his gown. The ship derives its origin from the seal of Stephen Payne who was Lord High Almoner to King Henry V from 1414 to 1419 when he was Dean of Exeter.*

FRONT COVER: *The Queen and the Duke of Edinburgh with the Secretary of the Royal Almonry and Children of the Royal Almonry outside Birmingham Cathedral.*

BACK COVER: *Yeomen of the Guard carrying the two dishes containing the traditional red and white long-stringed purses.*